VEGAN
FOR SENIORS

Dr. Kimberly Carlos

TABLE OF CONTENT

INTRODUCTION

Once upon a time in a quaint little town, there lived an elderly gentleman named Mr. Johnson. He had a passion for gardening and spent most of his days tending to his beautiful vegetable patch.

However, as the years passed, he faced health challenges, and his doctor recommended a renal diet to support his kidney function.

Mr. Johnson was determined to maintain his love for gardening and continue living a vibrant life. So, he decided to explore the world of vegan cuisine, which he believed could align with his renal diet requirements.

He embarked on a journey to learn all about vegan recipes that were suitable for seniors with kidney concerns.

With the help of local nutritionists and some internet research, he soon discovered a treasure trove of delicious, kidney-friendly vegan meals.

Armed with newfound knowledge, Mr. Johnson began experimenting in his kitchen.

He swapped traditional ingredients with plant-based alternatives, finding creative ways to add flavor without compromising on nutrition. His dishes included hearty vegetable stews, protein-rich quinoa salads, and flavorful tofu stir-fries.

As he delved deeper into the world of vegan renal cuisine, Mr. Johnson's health began to improve. His energy levels increased, and he felt more active than he had in years.

Not only did his kidneys respond positively to the diet, but he also experienced an overall sense of well-being.

Word of Mr. Johnson's success spread through the town, capturing the attention of other seniors facing similar health challenges.

Soon, he found himself hosting cooking workshops, sharing his knowledge and passion for the vegan renal diet with others. It became a delightful community gathering, where seniors exchanged stories, laughter, and delicious plant-based meals.

Mr. Johnson's garden became more bountiful than ever, producing an abundance of fresh, organic vegetables for his culinary creations. The community started to affectionately refer to him as "The Vegan Green Thumb."

In time, his humble kitchen workshops evolved into a thriving community initiative. Volunteers joined in, offering support and expanding the reach of the program to neighboring towns.

What started as one man's personal journey transformed into a movement promoting health and sustainability for seniors.

As the years passed, Mr. Johnson's legacy grew, and the benefits of the vegan renal diet for seniors became widely recognized. The town's seniors were healthier, happier, and united by the love of wholesome, plant-based cuisine.

And so, in this charming little town, Mr. Johnson's passion for gardening and his determination to overcome health challenges led to the blossoming of a compassionate community, showing that with a dash of love and a sprinkle of dedication, anyone can make a positive impact on the world around them.

CHAPTER ONE

Vegan Renal Diet for Seniors Diet and Benefits

As our bodies age, it becomes increasingly important to pay attention to our dietary choices, especially when facing health challenges like kidney concerns. For seniors, adopting a vegan renal diet can be a game-changer in maintaining optimal health, vitality, and overall well-being.

This book aims to explore the benefits of a vegan renal diet for seniors and provide practical tips on how to follow this diet to achieve positive outcomes.

Understanding the Vegan Renal Diet

The vegan renal diet combines the principles of a plant-based diet with specific guidelines to support kidney function. This diet focuses on consuming whole, unprocessed plant foods, while limiting certain nutrients that may strain the kidneys, such as sodium, phosphorus, and potassium. By adhering to these dietary restrictions, seniors can manage their kidney health effectively and reduce the risk of complications.

Benefits of the Vegan Renal Diet for Seniors

1. Improved Kidney Function: By adopting a vegan renal diet, seniors can reduce the workload on their kidneys, which may lead to improved kidney function and slower decline over time. Plant-based foods are generally lower in phosphorus and sodium, promoting kidney health.

2. Heart Health: Vegan diets have been linked to a reduced risk of heart disease. By avoiding animal products and consuming more fruits, vegetables, and whole grains, seniors can maintain a healthy heart, an essential aspect of overall well-being.

3. Weight Management: A well-balanced vegan renal diet can support weight management, which is crucial for seniors as excess weight can exacerbate kidney issues and other health conditions.

4. Digestive Health: The fiber-rich nature of plant-based foods can aid in maintaining a healthy digestive system, preventing constipation, and promoting gut health.

5. Lower Blood Pressure: A vegan renal diet, particularly low in sodium, can help lower blood pressure, reducing the risk of hypertension-related complications.

6. Nutrient-Rich Diet: Plant-based foods are abundant in essential vitamins, minerals, and antioxidants, supporting the body's immune system and overall nutritional needs.

Tips for Following a Vegan Renal Diet for Seniors

1. Consult with a Healthcare Professional: Before making any significant dietary changes, seniors should consult with their healthcare provider or a registered dietitian. They can provide personalized advice and ensure the diet aligns with individual health needs.

2. Focus on Plant-Based Proteins: Seniors can obtain adequate protein by incorporating legumes (beans, lentils, and peas), tofu, tempeh, and plant-based protein powders into their meals.

3. Limit Phosphorus-Rich Foods: Reduce intake of phosphorus-rich foods like dairy products, processed foods, nuts, and certain whole grains. Opt for lower-phosphorus alternatives such as white rice, cauliflower, and apples.

4. Manage Potassium Intake: Seniors should monitor potassium levels by limiting high-potassium foods like bananas, oranges, potatoes, and tomatoes. Instead, choose lower-potassium options like berries, cucumbers, and green beans.

5. Cook at Home: Preparing meals at home gives seniors better control over their ingredients and helps avoid hidden sodium and phosphorus found in many processed foods.

6. Stay Hydrated: Adequate hydration is essential for kidney health. Seniors should aim to drink plenty of water throughout the day, unless their healthcare provider advises otherwise.

CHAPTER TWO

14 Day Vegan Renal Diet for Seniors Diet Meal Plan

DAY 1

- Breakfast: Quinoa Porridge with Almond Milk, Chopped Apples, and Cinnamon
- Snack: Carrot Sticks with Hummus
- Lunch: Lentil and Vegetable Soup with a Side of Mixed Greens Salad (Use lemon juice and olive oil for dressing)
- Snack: Fresh Berries (Strawberries, Blueberries, or Raspberries)
- Dinner: Baked Tofu with Steamed Broccoli and Quinoa

DAY 2

- Breakfast: Oatmeal with Sliced Banana and a Drizzle of Maple Syrup
- Snack: Rice Cakes with Avocado Slices
- Lunch: Brown Rice Salad with Cucumber, Red Bell Pepper, and Chickpeas
- Snack: Sliced Mango
- Dinner: Vegetable Stir-Fry with Tofu over Cauliflower Rice

DAY 3

- Breakfast: Smoothie with Spinach, Pineapple, Banana, and Chia Seeds
- Snack: Sliced Cucumber with Guacamole
- Lunch: Zucchini Noodles with Tomato Sauce and Basil
- Snack: Melon Cubes (Watermelon, Cantaloupe, or Honeydew)
- Dinner: Baked Eggplant with Quinoa and a Side of Steamed Asparagus

DAY 4

- Breakfast: Vegan Pancakes with Fresh Berries and a Drizzle of Agave Syrup
- Snack: Celery Sticks with Peanut Butter
- Lunch: Chickpea and Spinach Salad with Balsamic Vinaigrette
- Snack: Orange Slices
- Dinner: Stuffed Bell Peppers with Brown Rice, Black Beans, and Salsa

DAY 5

- Breakfast: Chia Seed Pudding with Coconut Milk and Sliced Kiwi
- Snack: Rice Cakes with Sunflower Seed Butter
- Lunch: Burrito Bowl with Quinoa and Black Beans with Salsa and Avocado
- Snack: Fresh Pineapple Chunks
- Dinner: Baked Portobello Mushrooms with Sweet Potato Mash

DAY 6

- Breakfast: Smoothie Bowl with Acai, Mixed Berries, and Granola Topping
- Snack: Edamame Pods
- Lunch: Lentil and Kale Salad with Lemon-Tahini Dressing
- Snack: Apple Slices with Cinnamon
- Dinner: Vegan Lentil Shepherd's Pie with Mashed Cauliflower

DAY 7

- Breakfast: Overnight Oats with Almond Milk, Chopped Peaches, and Walnuts
- Snack: Cherry Tomatoes with Balsamic Glaze
- Lunch: Spinach and Arugula Salad with Roasted Beets and Orange Segments
- Snack: Grapes
- Dinner: Coconut Curry with Tofu and Mixed Vegetables over Quinoa

DAY 8

- Breakfast: Quinoa Porridge with Almond Milk, Chopped Apples, and Cinnamon
- Snack: Carrot Sticks with Hummus
- Lunch: Lentil and Vegetable Soup with a Side of Mixed Greens Salad (Use lemon juice and olive oil for dressing)
- Snack: Fresh Berries (Strawberries, Blueberries, or Raspberries)
- Dinner: Baked Tofu with Steamed Broccoli and Quinoa

DAY 9

- Breakfast: Oatmeal with Sliced Banana and a Drizzle of Maple Syrup
- Snack: Rice Cakes with Avocado Slices
- Lunch: Brown Rice Salad with Cucumber, Red Bell Pepper, and Chickpeas
- Snack: Sliced Mango
- Dinner: Vegetable Stir-Fry with Tofu over Cauliflower Rice

DAY 10

- Breakfast: Smoothie with Spinach, Pineapple, Banana, and Chia Seeds
- Snack: Sliced Cucumber with Guacamole
- Lunch: Zucchini Noodles with Tomato Sauce and Basil
- Snack: Melon Cubes (Watermelon, Cantaloupe, or Honeydew)
- Dinner: Baked Eggplant with Quinoa and a Side of Steamed Asparagus

DAY 11

- Breakfast: Vegan Pancakes with Fresh Berries and a Drizzle of Agave Syrup
- Snack: Celery Sticks with Peanut Butter
- Lunch: Chickpea and Spinach Salad with Balsamic Vinaigrette
- Snack: Orange Slices
- Dinner: Stuffed Bell Peppers with Brown Rice, Black Beans, and Salsa

DAY 12

- Breakfast: Chia Seed Pudding with Coconut Milk and Sliced Kiwi
- Snack: Rice Cakes with Sunflower Seed Butter
- Lunch: Burrito Bowl with Quinoa and Black Beans with Salsa and Avocado
- Snack: Fresh Pineapple Chunks
- Dinner: Baked Portobello Mushrooms with Sweet Potato Mash

DAY 13

- Breakfast: Smoothie Bowl with Acai, Mixed Berries, and Granola Topping
- Snack: Edamame Pods
- Lunch: Lentil and Kale Salad with Lemon-Tahini Dressing
- Snack: Apple Slices with Cinnamon
- Dinner: Vegan Lentil Shepherd's Pie with Mashed Cauliflower

DAY 14

- Breakfast: Overnight Oats with Almond Milk, Chopped Peaches, and Walnuts
- Snack: Cherry Tomatoes with Balsamic Glaze
- Lunch: Spinach and Arugula Salad with Roasted Beets and Orange Segments
- Snack: Grapes
- Dinner: Coconut Curry with Tofu and Mixed Vegetables over Quinoa

CHAPTER THREE

Vegan Renal Diet for Seniors Diet Breakfast Recipes

1. Vegan Blueberry Almond Smoothie Bowl

Ingredients:

- 1 cup frozen blueberries
- 1 ripe banana
- 1 tablespoon almond butter
- 1 cup unsweetened almond milk
- 2 tablespoons chia seeds
- Fresh blueberries and sliced almonds for topping

Instructions:

1. In a blender, combine the frozen blueberries, ripe banana, almond butter, and almond milk.
2. Blend until smooth and creamy.
3. Pour the smoothie into a bowl and sprinkle chia seeds on top.
4. Add fresh blueberries and sliced almonds as a delightful garnish.
5. Enjoy immediately.

Cooking Time: 5 minutes

2. Quinoa Breakfast Porridge

Ingredients:

- 1/2 cup quinoa, rinsed
- 1 cup unsweetened almond milk
- 1/2 teaspoon ground cinnamon
- 1 tablespoon maple syrup
- Chopped fresh fruits (e.g., peaches, berries) and nuts for topping

Instructions:

1. Combine the quinoa, almond milk, and cinnamon in a small saucepan.

2. Bring to a boil, then reduce heat and simmer for 15-20 minutes or until quinoa is cooked and the mixture thickens.

3. Stir in the maple syrup and adjust sweetness to taste.

4. Serve the quinoa porridge in bowls and top with chopped fresh fruits and nuts.

5. Savor the comforting and kidney-friendly breakfast.

Cooking Time: 20 minutes

3. Vegan Avocado Toast with Tomato

Ingredients:

- 2 slices whole-grain bread (low-sodium if possible)
- 1 ripe avocado
- 1 medium tomato, sliced
- Fresh lemon juice
- Salt and pepper to taste

Instructions:

1. Toast the whole-grain bread slices to desired crispness.

2. Mash the ripe avocado in a bowl and season with fresh lemon juice, salt, and pepper.

3. Spread the avocado mixture generously on each toast.

4. Top with sliced tomatoes for a burst of freshness.

5. Serve immediately and relish the simple and kidney-friendly flavors.

Cooking Time: 10 minutes

4. Vegan Tofu Scramble

Ingredients:

- 1/2 block firm tofu, crumbled
- 1 tablespoon nutritional yeast
- 1/2 teaspoon ground turmeric
- 1/4 teaspoon garlic powder
- 1/4 teaspoon onion powder
- 1/2 cup diced bell peppers
- 1/2 cup baby spinach leaves
- Salt and pepper to taste

Instructions:

1. In a non-stick skillet, sauté the crumbled tofu over medium heat until slightly golden.
2. Add nutritional yeast, ground turmeric, garlic powder, and onion powder to the tofu. Mix well to coat evenly.
3. Stir in diced bell peppers and baby spinach leaves, cooking until the vegetables are tender.
4. Season with salt and pepper according to taste preferences.
5. Serve the flavorful tofu scramble on a plate, ready to be enjoyed.

Cooking Time: 15 minutes

5. Vegan Banana Walnut Muffins

Ingredients:

- 1 1/2 cups whole wheat flour
- 1/2 cup almond flour
- 1 teaspoon baking powder
- 1/2 teaspoon baking soda
- 1/4 teaspoon salt
- 1/2 cup mashed ripe bananas
- 1/3 cup maple syrup
- 1/4 cup unsweetened applesauce
- 1/2 cup unsweetened almond milk
- 1 teaspoon vanilla extract
- 1/2 cup chopped walnuts

Instructions:

1. Set the oven's temperature to 350°F (175°C). A muffin pan should be lined with paper liners.

2. Combine whole wheat flour, almond flour, baking powder, baking soda, and salt in a large bowl.

3. Combine mashed bananas, maple syrup, applesauce, almond milk, and vanilla extract in another bowl.

4. Stirring gently to incorporate, gradually add the wet components to the dry ingredients.

5. Stir the chopped walnuts into the mixture for the muffins.

6. Divide the batter among the muffin tins in an even fashion.

7. Bake for 18-20 minutes or until a toothpick inserted in the center comes out clean.

8. After the muffins have cooled in the pan for five minutes, move them to a wire rack to finish cooling.

Cooking Time: 30 minutes

Vegan Renal Diet for Seniors Diet Lunch Recipes

1. Lentil and Vegetable Soup

Ingredients:

- 1 cup washed green or brown lentils
- 4 cups low-sodium vegetable broth
- 1 medium carrot, diced
- 1 celery stalk, diced
- 1/2 cup diced zucchini

- 1/2 cup chopped spinach
- 1 teaspoon dried thyme
- 1 bay leaf
- Salt and pepper to taste

Instructions:

1. In a large pot, combine the lentils, vegetable broth, carrot, celery, zucchini, dried thyme, and bay leaf.

2. After the mixture comes to a boil, lower the heat and simmer the stew for 20 to 25 minutes, or until the lentils are cooked through.

3. Stir in the chopped spinach and cook for an additional 2-3 minutes until wilted.

4. Season with salt and pepper according to taste preferences.

5. Remove the bay leaf and serve the hearty lentil and vegetable soup hot.

Cooking Time: 30 minutes

2. Chickpea and Quinoa Salad

Ingredients:

- 1 cup cooked quinoa
- 1 can (15 oz) washed and drained chickpeas
- 1/2 cucumber, diced
- 1/2 red bell pepper, diced
- 1/4 cup chopped fresh parsley
- 2 tablespoons lemon juice
- 2 tablespoons olive oil
- Salt and pepper to taste

Instructions:

1. In a large mixing bowl, combine cooked quinoa, chickpeas, diced cucumber, red bell pepper, and chopped parsley.
2. In a separate small bowl, whisk together lemon juice, olive oil, salt, and pepper to create the dressing.
3. Drizzle the dressing over the salad and toss gently to combine all the ingredients.
4. Adjust seasoning as needed.
5. Serve the refreshing chickpea and quinoa salad at room temperature or chilled.

Cooking Time: 20 minutes (if quinoa is pre-cooked)

3. Vegan Lentil Shepherd's Pie

Ingredients:

- cooked green or brown lentils, 1 cup
- 1 cup diced carrots
- 1 cup peas (fresh or frozen)
- 1/2 cup diced onions
- 2 cloves garlic, minced
- 2 tablespoons tomato paste
- 1 tablespoon low-sodium soy sauce
- 1/2 cup low-sodium vegetable broth
- 3 cups mashed sweet potatoes (cooked and mashed)
- Salt and pepper to taste

Instructions:

1. Preheat the oven to 375°F (190°C).

2. In a large skillet, sauté diced onions and minced garlic until translucent.

3. Add diced carrots and peas to the skillet and cook until slightly tender.

4. Stir in the cooked lentils, tomato paste, low-sodium soy sauce, and vegetable broth. Mix well and simmer for 5-7 minutes until the mixture thickens.

5. Transfer the lentil filling to a baking dish and spread the mashed sweet potatoes evenly on top.

6. Bake in the preheated oven for 20-25 minutes or until the sweet potato topping is lightly browned.

7. Let it cool for a few minutes before serving the comforting vegan lentil shepherd's pie.

Cooking Time: 45 minutes (if sweet potatoes are pre-cooked)

4. Tofu and Vegetable Stir-Fry

Ingredients:

- 1 block firm tofu, cubed
- 2 cups mixed stir-fry vegetables (broccoli, bell peppers, snap peas, etc.)
- 2 tablespoons low-sodium soy sauce
- 1 tablespoon maple syrup
- 1 tablespoon sesame oil
- 1 teaspoon grated ginger
- 2 cloves garlic, minced
- Sesame seeds for garnish

Instructions:

1. Heat the sesame oil in a sizable skillet or wok over medium heat.

2. Add the cubed tofu and cook until lightly browned on all sides.

3. Stir in the mixed vegetables, grated ginger, and minced garlic. Sauté for an additional 3-4 minutes until the vegetables are tender-crisp.

4. In a small bowl, whisk together low-sodium soy sauce and maple syrup to create the sauce.

5. Pour the sauce over the tofu and vegetable mixture, tossing to coat evenly.

6. Cook for another minute until the sauce thickens slightly.

7. Garnish with sesame seeds before serving the flavorful tofu and vegetable stir-fry.

Cooking Time: 20 minutes

5. Zucchini Noodles with Tomato Sauce

Ingredients:

- 2 large zucchinis, spiralized into noodles
- 1 can (15 oz) crushed tomatoes (no salt added)
- 1 tablespoon olive oil
- 1 teaspoon dried oregano
- 1/2 teaspoon garlic powder
- 1/4 teaspoon optional red pepper flakes, crushed
- Fresh basil leaves for garnish
- Salt and pepper to taste

Instructions:

1. Heat the olive oil in a saucepan over medium heat.
2. Include crushed tomatoes, dried oregano, crushed red pepper flakes (if using), and garlic powder. For the flavors to combine, simmer for 5-7 minutes.
3. In a separate large pan, sauté zucchini noodles for 1-2 minutes until slightly softened.
4. Season the zucchini noodles with salt and pepper to taste.
5. Pour the tomato sauce over the zucchini noodles and toss to combine.
6. Garnish with fresh basil leaves before serving the light and delightful zucchini noodles with tomato sauce.

Cooking Time: 15 minutes

CHAPTER FOUR

Vegan Renal Diet for Seniors Diet Dinner Recipes

1. Baked Eggplant with Quinoa

Ingredients:

- 1 medium eggplant, sliced
- 1 cup cooked quinoa
- One (15 oz) can of chopped tomatoes without salt
- 1 tablespoon olive oil
- 1 teaspoon dried basil
- 1/2 teaspoon garlic powder
- Salt and pepper to taste

Instructions:

1. Preheat the oven to 375°F (190°C).
2. Arrange the eggplant slices on a baking pan and drizzle both sides with olive oil.
3. Bake the eggplant slices in the preheated oven for 15-20 minutes or until tender.
4. In a saucepan, combine the diced tomatoes, dried basil, garlic powder, salt, and pepper. Simmer for 5-

7 minutes until the flavors meld.

5. Serve the baked eggplant slices over cooked quinoa and top with the tomato sauce.

6. Enjoy this nutritious and kidney-friendly dinner.

Cooking Time: 30 minutes (including quinoa cooking time)

2. Vegan Lentil Chili

Ingredients:

- 1 cup washed green or brown lentils
- One (15 oz) can of chopped tomatoes without salt
- 1 can (15 oz) rinsed and drained low-sodium kidney beans
- 1 cup diced bell peppers
- 1 cup diced onions
- 2 cloves garlic, minced
- 2 tablespoons chili powder
- 1 teaspoon ground cumin
- 4 cups low-sodium vegetable broth
- Fresh cilantro for garnish
- Salt and pepper to taste

Instructions:

1. In a large pot, sauté diced onions and minced garlic until translucent.

2. Add diced bell peppers to the pot and cook for another 2-3 minutes.

3. Stir in lentils, diced tomatoes, kidney beans, chili powder, ground cumin, and vegetable broth.

4. Bring the mixture to a boil, then reduce heat and simmer for 25-30 minutes or until the lentils are tender.

5. Season with salt and pepper according to taste preferences.

6. Garnish with fresh cilantro before serving the hearty and kidney-friendly vegan lentil chili.

Cooking Time: 40 minutes

3. Black beans and quinoa stuffed bell peppers

Ingredients:

- 1 cup cooked quinoa
- 4 large bell peppers, any color, tops removed and

seeds thrown out

- 1 can (15 oz) black beans with minimal sodium, drained, and rinsed
- 1 cup diced tomatoes (no salt added)
- 1/2 cup diced onions
- 2 cloves garlic, minced
- 1 teaspoon ground cumin
- 1/2 teaspoon chili powder
- 1/4 cup chopped fresh cilantro
- Salt and pepper to taste

Instructions:

1. Preheat the oven to 375°F (190°C).

2. In a large skillet, sauté diced onions and minced garlic until translucent.

3. Stir in diced tomatoes, black beans, ground cumin, and chili powder. Cook for another 3-4 minutes.

4. Include the cooked quinoa and freshly cut cilantro in the skillet. Add salt and pepper after thoroughly combining.

5. Place the bell peppers in a baking tray after stuffing them with the mixture.

6. Bake the peppers in the preheated oven for 25 to 30 minutes, or until they are soft.

7. Serve the flavorful stuffed bell peppers hot.

Cooking Time: 40 minutes (including quinoa cooking time)

4. Coconut Curry with Tofu and Vegetables

Ingredients:

- 1 block firm tofu, cubed
- 1 cup chopped mixed vegetables (carrots, bell peppers, snap peas, etc.)
- 1 can (13.5 oz) coconut milk (unsweetened)
- 2 tablespoons red curry paste
- 1 tablespoon low-sodium soy sauce
- 1 tablespoon coconut oil
- Garnish: wedges of lime and fresh cilantro
- Salt and pepper to taste

Instructions:

1. In a large skillet or wok, heat coconut oil over medium heat.
2. Add cubed tofu and sauté until lightly browned on all sides.

3. Stir in chopped mixed vegetables and cook until tender-crisp.
4. Add red curry paste and low-sodium soy sauce to the skillet, mixing well with the tofu and vegetables.
5. Pour in the coconut milk and simmer for 5-7 minutes until the flavors meld and the curry thickens slightly.
6. Season with salt and pepper according to taste preferences.
7. Garnish with fresh cilantro and lime wedges before serving the delectable coconut curry with tofu and vegetables.

Cooking Time: 25 minutes

5. Vegan enchiladas with sweet potatoes and black beans

Ingredients:

- 1 large sweet potato, chopped after being peeled
- 1 can (15 oz) low-sodium black beans, drained and rinsed
- 1 cup diced onions
- 2 cloves garlic, minced
- 1 teaspoon ground cumin
- 1/2 teaspoon chili powder
- 1 can (15 oz) enchilada sauce (no salt added)

- 8 small whole-grain tortillas
- Slices of fresh cilantro and avocado as garnish
- Salt and pepper to taste

Instructions:

1. Preheat the oven to 375°F (190°C).
2. In a large skillet, sauté diced onions and minced garlic until translucent.
3. Add diced sweet potatoes to the skillet and cook until tender.
4. Stir in black beans, ground cumin, and chili powder. Cook for another 2-3 minutes.
5. Pour half of the enchilada sauce into a baking dish.
6. Fill each tortilla with the sweet potato and black bean mixture, rolling them up, and place them seam side down in the baking dish.
7. Pour the remaining enchilada sauce over the rolled tortillas.
8. Bake in the preheated oven for 20-25 minutes or until the enchiladas are heated through.
9. Garnish with fresh cilantro and avocado slices before serving the delightful vegan sweet potato and black bean enchiladas.

Cooking Time: 40 minutes

Vegan Renal Diet for Seniors Diet Dessert Recipes

1. Chia Seed Pudding with Fresh Berries

Ingredients:

- 1/4 cup chia seeds
- 1 1/2 cups unsweetened almond milk
- 1 tablespoon maple syrup (or your preferred sweetener)
- 1 teaspoon vanilla extract
- Fresh berries for topping (e.g., strawberries, blueberries)

Instructions:

1. In a bowl, mix chia seeds, unsweetened almond milk, maple syrup, and vanilla extract.
2. Give the chia seeds a good stir to spread them evenly.
3. Cover the bowl and refrigerate for at least 2 hours or overnight until the mixture thickens and forms a pudding-like consistency.
4. Before serving, top the chia seed pudding with fresh berries for added sweetness and antioxidants.
5. Enjoy the creamy and guilt-free chia seed pudding.

Cooking Time: 2 hours (mainly for refrigeration)

2. Baked Apples with Cinnamon and Almonds

Ingredients:

- 2 medium apples, cored and halved
- 1 tablespoon maple syrup
- 1 teaspoon ground cinnamon
- 2 tablespoons chopped almonds

Instructions:

1. Preheat the oven to 375°F (190°C).

2. Place the halved apples on a baking sheet, cut side up.

3. Drizzle maple syrup over the apples and sprinkle with ground cinnamon.

4. Bake the apples in the preheated oven for 20-25 minutes or until tender.

5. Sprinkle chopped almonds over the baked apples before serving.

6. Savor the warm and comforting baked apples with a delightful nutty crunch.

Cooking Time: 25 minutes

3. Vegan Banana Nice Cream

Ingredients:

- 2 ripe bananas, sliced and frozen
- 1/4 cup unsweetened almond milk
- 1 teaspoon vanilla extract
- Toppings of choice (e.g., chopped nuts, dark chocolate chips, coconut flakes)

Instructions:

1. In a blender or food processor, blend the frozen banana slices, almond milk, and vanilla extract until smooth and creamy.

2. Transfer the nice cream to a bowl and add your favorite toppings for extra texture and flavor.

3. Serve the creamy and guilt-free vegan banana nice cream immediately.

4. Enjoy a healthy and cooling dessert without any added sugars.

Preparation Time: 10 minutes

4. Vegan Rice Pudding with Cinnamon

Ingredients:

- 1 cup cooked white rice
- 1 1/2 cups unsweetened almond milk
- 2 tablespoons maple syrup
- 1 teaspoon ground cinnamon
- 1/4 teaspoon ground nutmeg
- 1/4 cup raisins (optional)

Instructions:

1. In a saucepan, combine cooked white rice, unsweetened almond milk, maple syrup, ground cinnamon, and ground nutmeg.
2. Cook over medium heat, stirring occasionally, until the mixture thickens and resembles a creamy pudding.
3. If using raisins, stir them into the rice pudding before serving.
4. Sprinkle a pinch of ground cinnamon on top for an extra hint of flavor.
5. Serve the warm and comforting vegan rice pudding.

Cooking Time: 15 minutes

5. Vegan Berry Parfait

Ingredients:

- One cup of mixed berries, including strawberries, blueberries, and raspberries.
- 1 cup vegan yogurt (low-sugar if possible)
- 1/4 cup granola (low-sugar if possible)
- Fresh mint leaves for garnish (optional)

Instructions:

1. In a serving glass or bowl, layer mixed berries, vegan yogurt, and granola.

2. Continue layering the glass until it is full.

3. Garnish with fresh mint leaves for a delightful pop of color and flavor.

4. Refrigerate the vegan berry parfait for 30 minutes to allow the flavors to meld before serving.

5. Enjoy this refreshing and kidney-friendly dessert parfait.

Cooking Time: 5 minutes

CHAPTER FIVE

Vegan Renal Diet for Seniors Diet Snacks Recipes

1. Carrot and Cucumber Sticks with Hummus

Ingredients:

- 2 medium carrots, cut into sticks
- 1 medium cucumber, cut into sticks
- 1/2 cup homemade or store-bought low-sodium hummus

Instructions:

1. Wash and peel the carrots and cucumber.

2. Cut them into sticks for easy snacking.

3. Serve the carrot and cucumber sticks with a side of low-sodium hummus for a delightful and crunchy snack.

4. Dip the veggies into the hummus and enjoy the nutrient-rich and kidney-friendly combination.

Preparation Time: 10 minutes

2. Rice Cakes with Avocado and Sprouts

Ingredients:

- 4 rice cakes (low-sodium if possible)
- 1 ripe avocado, sliced
- 1/2 cup fresh sprouts (e.g., alfalfa, broccoli)
- 1 teaspoon lemon juice
- Salt and pepper to taste

Instructions:

1. Arrange the rice cakes on a serving plate.

2. Place avocado slices on each rice cake, gently mashing them with a fork.

3. Drizzle lemon juice over the avocado and season with salt and pepper.

4. Top the avocado with a generous amount of fresh sprouts.

5. Savor the light and refreshing rice cakes with avocado and sprouts.

Preparation Time: 10 minutes

3. Edamame Guacamole with Baked Tortilla Chips

Ingredients:

- 1 cup shelled edamame (cooked and cooled)
- 1 ripe avocado
- 1/4 cup diced red onion
- 1 clove garlic, minced
- 1 tablespoon lime juice
- Salt and pepper to taste
- Baked whole-grain tortilla chips (low-sodium if possible)

Instructions:

1. In a food processor, blend the shelled edamame, avocado, diced red onion, minced garlic, and lime juice until smooth and creamy.

2. Season with salt and pepper according to taste preferences.

3. To allow the flavors to mingle, transfer the edamame guacamole to a serving bowl and place in the refrigerator for 30 minutes.

4. Serve the guacamole with baked whole-grain tortilla chips for a satisfying and kidney-friendly snack.

Preparation Time: 15 minutes

4. Celery Sticks with Peanut Butter

Ingredients:

- 4 large celery stalks, cut into sticks
- 1/4 cup natural peanut butter (no added sugars or salt)

Instructions:

1. Wash and cut the celery stalks into sticks.

2. Spread peanut butter on each celery stick.

3. Enjoy the crisp and crunchy celery sticks with the creamy and nutty peanut butter for a wholesome and kidney-friendly snack.

Preparation Time: 5 minutes

5. Fresh Fruit Salad

Ingredients:

- 1 cup mixed fresh fruits (e.g., strawberries, blueberries, kiwi, melon)
- 1 tablespoon fresh lemon juice
- Fresh mint leaves for garnish (optional)

Instructions:

1. Wash and prepare the fresh fruits by cutting them into bite-sized pieces.

2. In a mixing bowl, toss the mixed fruits with fresh lemon juice to prevent browning and add a zesty flavor.

3. Garnish the fruit salad with fresh mint leaves for an extra pop of freshness and color.

4. Serve the refreshing and nutrient-rich fruit salad as a light and hydrating snack.

Preparation Time: 10 minutes

Vegan Renal Diet for Seniors Diet Smoothies and Juicing Recipes

1. Berry Beet Smoothie

Ingredients:

- One cup of mixed berries, including strawberries, blueberries, and raspberries.
- 1 cup unsweetened almond milk - 1 small cooked beet that has been peeled and diced
- 1 tbsp. chia seeds
- A teaspoon of maple syrup, if desired, for sweetness

Instructions:

1. In a blender, combine mixed berries, cooked beet, unsweetened almond milk, and chia seeds.

2. Blend until smooth and creamy.

3. If desired, add maple syrup for extra sweetness.

4. Pour the berry beet smoothie into a glass and enjoy the vibrant and kidney-friendly beverage.

Preparation Time: 5 minutes

2. Green Kale and Cucumber Juice

Ingredients:

- 2 cups chopped (stems removed) kale leaves
- 1 medium cucumber, peeled and chopped
- 1 green apple, cored and chopped
- 1-inch piece of ginger, peeled
- 1 tablespoon lemon juice

Instructions:

1. Using a juicer, process the chopped kale, cucumber, green apple, and ginger to extract the juice.

2. Stir in lemon juice for a zesty kick.

3. Serve the green kale and cucumber juice immediately for a refreshing and nutrient-rich drink.

Preparation Time: 10 minutes

3. Tropical Turmeric Smoothie

Ingredients:

- 1 cup fresh or frozen diced pineapple
- 1 ripe banana

- 1/2 cup fresh or frozen mango dice
- 1 cup coconut water
- 1/2 teaspoon ground turmeric
- 1 tablespoon ground flaxseed (optional for added fiber)

Instructions:

1. In a blender, combine diced pineapple, ripe banana, diced mango, coconut water, and ground turmeric.

2. Blend until smooth and creamy.

3. If desired, add ground flaxseed for extra fiber.

4. Pour the tropical turmeric smoothie into a glass and relish the delightful and kidney-friendly flavors.

Preparation Time: 5 minutes

4. Watermelon Cucumber Cooler

Ingredients:

- 2 cups diced seedless watermelon
- 1 small cucumber, peeled and chopped
- 1 tablespoon fresh lime juice
- Fresh mint leaves for garnish

Instructions:

1. In a blender, combine diced watermelon, chopped cucumber, and fresh lime juice.

2. Blend until smooth and well combined.

3. Pour the watermelon cucumber cooler into a glass and garnish with fresh mint leaves.

4. Sip on this hydrating and kidney-friendly beverage for a cooling and refreshing experience.

Preparation Time: 5 minutes

5. Creamy Avocado Spinach Smoothie

Ingredients:

- 1 ripe avocado
- 1 cup packed baby spinach leaves
- 1 cup unsweetened almond milk
- 1 tablespoon almond butter
- A teaspoon of maple syrup, if desired, for sweetness

Instructions:

1. In a blender, combine the ripe avocado, baby spinach leaves, unsweetened almond milk, and almond butter.

2. Blend until smooth and creamy.

3. If desired, add maple syrup for extra sweetness.

4. Pour the creamy avocado spinach smoothie into a glass and enjoy the nourishing and kidney-friendly treat.

Preparation Time: 5 minutes

CONCLUSION

The Vegan Renal Diet for seniors is a powerful dietary approach that offers numerous benefits for kidney health and overall well-being.

By adopting a plant-based diet, seniors with kidney issues can significantly reduce the burden on their kidneys while enjoying a wide array of nutrient-rich and delicious foods.

Throughout this comprehensive exploration of the Vegan Renal Diet for seniors, we have delved into the principles, benefits, and numerous recipes designed to support kidney health.

The main focus of the diet is to minimize the intake of high-potassium, high-phosphorus, and high-sodium foods that can put strain on the kidneys.

Instead, the diet encourages a rich consumption of plant-based foods that are low in these harmful minerals, thereby aiding in the maintenance of kidney function and preventing further damage.

The benefits of the Vegan Renal Diet are multi-faceted.

Firstly, its emphasis on plant-based foods, such as fruits, vegetables, legumes, and whole grains, provides an abundance of vitamins, minerals, and antioxidants that promote overall health.

These nutrients also play a crucial role in supporting kidney function and reducing the risk of chronic diseases commonly associated with aging, such as hypertension, cardiovascular disease, and diabetes.

Secondly, the diet is lower in protein compared to traditional diets, which can be beneficial for seniors with kidney impairment. Reducing protein intake helps to alleviate the workload on the kidneys, as protein breakdown generates waste products that need to be filtered by these organs.

By choosing plant-based protein sources, such as beans, lentils, and tofu, seniors can maintain muscle mass and strength without overburdening their kidneys.

Furthermore, the Vegan Renal Diet is naturally low in saturated fats and cholesterol, promoting heart health and reducing the risk of atherosclerosis and related complications.

As a result, seniors can experience improved cardiovascular function, reduced blood pressure, and enhanced circulation, all of which are critical factors in maintaining healthy kidneys.

The recipes provided for breakfast, lunch, dinner, snacks, and desserts showcase the incredible diversity and flavors that a Vegan Renal Diet can offer. From colorful smoothie bowls to hearty lentil soups, each meal is carefully crafted to ensure seniors enjoy a delicious and satisfying culinary experience while adhering to the principles of kidney-friendly nutrition.

The Vegan Renal Diet is not without its challenges, as seniors may need to pay attention to their nutrient intake, especially with regard to vitamin B12, iron, calcium, and omega-3 fatty acids.

However, with proper planning and potentially supplementing when necessary, these challenges can be addressed effectively, ensuring seniors maintain a well-balanced and wholesome diet.

In conclusion, the Vegan Renal Diet for seniors offers a wealth of advantages for kidney health and overall vitality. By focusing on plant-based foods and reducing the intake of harmful minerals, seniors can protect and support their kidneys, while also reaping the benefits of a diet rich in essential nutrients and antioxidants.

The combination of delicious and nutritious recipes makes the transition to this diet enjoyable and sustainable, enhancing the quality of life for seniors as they age gracefully with optimal kidney function and well-being.

As with any significant dietary change, it is recommended that seniors consult with their healthcare provider or a registered dietitian to ensure that the Vegan Renal Diet aligns with their individual health needs and medical conditions.

By doing so, seniors can embark on a healthful and fulfilling journey towards kidney-friendly eating and a vibrant lifestyle.